* * * * * * * * * * * * * * * * * * * *

WHO ARE
THE HEROES OF
THE *CHALLENGER?*

* * * * * * * * * * * * * * * * * *
* * Gregory Jarvis *
* Christa McAuliffe *
* Ronald McNair *
* Ellison Onizuka *
* Judith Resnik *
* Francis "Dick" Scobee *
* Michael Smith *
* * * * * * * * * * * * * * * * * *

Heroes of the Challenger will tell you everything you want to know about these courageous space shuttle astronauts. It will also answer all your questions about the exciting future still waiting in America's largest frontier—space!

* * * * * * * * * * * * * * * * * * * *

HEROES
OF THE CHALLENGER

Daniel and Susan Cohen

Illustrated with photographs

AN ARCHWAY PAPERBACK
Published by POCKET BOOKS • NEW YORK

All photos, unless otherwise credited, are courtesy of NASA.

AN ARCHWAY PAPERBACK *Original*

An Archway Paperback published by
POCKET BOOKS, a division of Simon & Schuster, Inc.
1230 Avenue of the Americas, New York, N.Y. 10020

ISBN: 0-671-62948-4

First Archway Paperback printing July, 1986

10 9 8 7 6 5 4 3

AN ARCHWAY PAPERBACK and colophon are
registered trademarks of Simon & Schuster, Inc.

Printed in U.S.A.

IL 4+

Contents

HEROES

OF THE CHALLENGER

The *Challenger* crew the day before the disaster.
Crew members are, front to back: Francis "Dick"
Scobee, Judith Resnik, Ronald McNair, Michael
Smith, Christa McAuliffe, Ellison Onizuka, Gregory
Jarvis.

Chapter 1

JANUARY 28, 1986—
11:39.13 A.M.

The morning of Tuesday, January 28, 1986, is a time that you will probably remember for the rest of your life. You will be able to recall where you had been and what you were doing. That is when the space shuttle *Challenger* exploded.

For other generations there had been other awful moments that could not be forgotten. People remembered where they were when they first heard that Pearl Harbor was bombed on December 7, 1941, or where they were on November 22, 1963, when they first heard that President Kennedy was shot, or April 4, 1968, when they first heard of the shooting of Martin Luther King. For many young people the awful moment will be January 28, 1986.

It wasn't that older people didn't care about

the *Challenger*. We certainly did. But most of us had grown up with the space program, and had lived with it for a long time. We had anxiously watched the launchings of the Mercury astronauts back in the early 1960s. We had seen the successful Apollo missions to the moon in the late '60s. We had been glued to our TV sets for the first few launchings and landings of the space shuttle in the early 1980s.

But by 1986 we had, quite frankly, come to take the shuttle for granted. Sure, we all knew in a general sort of way that shuttle flights were not the same as ordinary airplane flights. We knew that the technology was still new and tremendously complicated. We also knew that the shuttle rode into space atop huge tanks of highly explosive fuel. In short, we knew that things could go disastrously, catastrophically wrong. We knew it, yet we didn't quite believe it. It seemed that there were so many precautions that a major failure was nearly impossible. Even if a little tiny thing seemed to be amiss, the flight was delayed or canceled altogether. There had already been a number of delays for this *Challenger* flight. Most of all, the shuttle program had become almost routine. There had already been 24 successful shuttle flights. Sure, there had been problems, even serious ones, but they could all be corrected, without anyone getting hurt. At least so we thought.

Most TV networks agreed that shuttle

launches had become routine and boring. They weren't big news any longer. None of the major networks covered the *Challenger* launch live. Only the Atlanta-based Cable News Network provided live television coverage. The launch was covered live by a number of radio stations. The networks planned to show a few minutes of tape of the launch on the evening news.

But for the young people of America, this shuttle flight was special. It was special because one of the seven aboard was a teacher named Christa McAuliffe. She was the first private citizen ever to go into space. She had been scheduled to teach several "lessons from space" that would be beamed directly into the nation's classrooms. Christa McAuliffe had been chosen specifically to build a stronger and more personal connection between the nation's students and the space program. As a result a far larger than usual percentage of students had studied about this shuttle and planned to watch the launching live from their classrooms and auditoriums.

It wasn't just Christa McAuliffe, however, that made this particular flight special—it was the whole crew. In the past the astronauts seemed rather remote figures. Most of them were military men and test pilots. They were heroic but not the sort of individuals that average Americans could readily identify with. In this respect the crew of the *Challenger* was quite different. The crew seemed to have been picked

3

to represent a broad cross section of America. They were men and women, of all races and religions and from a wide variety of backgrounds. They were the sort of people with whom all young Americans could easily identify. That is why this flight was so special, and why the tragedy is something that you will probably never forget. It was in many ways the most personal of all the U.S. space flights.

The *Challenger* had not been launched on schedule. It had been subjected to a series of irritating but not unusual delays. The original date for lift-off was January 20, but had slipped to Saturday January 25 because of delays in a previous mission with the space shuttle *Columbia*.

On Saturday, however, NASA learned there was a dust storm at the emergency landing facility in the African nation of Senegal. Such a facility would be used only if trouble developed before the shuttle had attained orbit. These emergency facilities—there are several of them —had never been used. But under NASA's tight safety rules the shuttle couldn't be launched unless it had somewhere to land before going into orbit. The flight was rescheduled for Sunday.

When Sunday morning dawned, it was raining at the Kennedy Space Center in Cape Canaveral, Florida. Rain can damage the shuttle's heat-resistant tiles. So the flight was delayed another 24 hours.

On Monday the weather had cleared. The crew boarded the shuttle and the countdown began. The countdown reached T (for takeoff) minus nine minutes, and then it stopped. A bolt had gotten stuck on a handle outside the craft. The handle had to be removed before the countdown could continue. Technicians called for a special drill, but when it finally arrived, the battery was dead and there were no replacements available. Finally an ordinary hacksaw was used to remove the bolt. The sight of technicians attacking one of the most sophisticated pieces of equipment in the world with a hacksaw was funny, and embarrassing to NASA, the National Aeronautics and Space Administration.

Worse still, the weather at the launch site had deteriorated. Winds of up to 35 mph were now whipping across the Kennedy Space Center. The winds would not have affected the launch itself. However, if something had gone wrong immediately after lift-off, it might have been possible for the shuttle itself to be released from the fuel tank and booster rockets and loop back to make a landing on the landing strip at the Space Center. This sort of emergency landing could not be accomplished in a stiff wind. So the flight was delayed once again. The repeated delays were very frustrating for the crew and for NASA officials. They also helped to create the impression that all possible sources of trouble were being monitored.

On Monday night the temperature fell to 26°F, unusually low for southern Florida even in January. Icicles formed all over the shuttle and launch pad. A special "ice team" from NASA went over the shuttle and found that the icicles had not damaged the heat-shield tiles. Still there was some concern over the temperature. Although temperatures were rising, they remained low that morning, lower than they had been for any previous shuttle launch. The winds, however, died down and the sky was a brilliant blue. Ultimately the decision to launch was made.

Challenger's crew, wearing gloves to ward off the chill, waved and smiled as they boarded the shuttle and took their assigned places. The countdown began. At any point during the countdown it could be stopped either by a decision from NASA controllers, or automatically if the computers which monitored thousands of functions aboard the shuttle sensed there was anything wrong. In June 1984 a shuttle launch had been stopped just four minutes before the main engines were to ignite when the computer sensed that one of the four engines was not delivering the proper thrust. Often it seemed that launches were stopped for trivial reasons, or simply because the computer or one of its sensors made an error. People outside the space program sometimes wondered if NASA wasn't being too careful. But this time everything seemed to be going smoothly.

NASA communicator Hugh Harris broadcast the countdown over a public-address system to the thousand or so spectators who had gathered to watch the lift-off. His voice was also heard over TV and radio.

"Four . . . three . . . two . . . one . . . and lift-off. Lift-off of the 25th space shuttle mission. And it has cleared the tower."

The launch looked perfect. No one on the ground was able to observe a small but ominous puff of black smoke from the right booster rocket.

After lift-off, public announcement of the flight's progress was taken over by Commander Steve Nesbitt, the communicator at the Johnson Space Center at Houston, Texas. Nesbitt, of course, could not see what was actually happening. He was not even looking at a televised picture of the launch. He was looking at data sent in by the computers to the main spaceflight center. Everything seemed normal, and that is what his announcements indicated.

Aboard the shuttle itself none of the astronauts was aware anything was wrong. Just 16 seconds after lift-off, Commander Francis Scobee communicated with the flight controllers,

"Houston, we have roll program." That meant that the shuttle turned to assume the proper position for entering orbit. It was all perfectly normal and "by the book."

About half a minute into the flight, the *Challenger*'s engines were throttled back to 65 percent of full power, which was perfectly normal.

A little under a minute into the flight, *Challenger* was told to go "throttle up" to reach "104 percent of power." The *Challenger*'s engines were slightly more powerful than previous engines, so they were actually able to produce 4 percent more power than the old standard. This increase in power was accomplished automatically. At that point the *Challenger* was going through the period of greatest stress during the ascent. Yet everything seemed perfectly normal on the ground and in the shuttle itself.

"Roger, go with throttle up," said Commander Scobee, 70 seconds into the flight.

Later, long-range television pictures were to show an orange glow, a flame of some sort, between the orbiter itself and the huge liquid-fuel tank which was to provide most of the power to put the shuttle into orbit. None of this was visible to people on the ground, nor was there any hint that anything was amiss in the data that was pouring into the Johnson Space Center in Houston. Commander Nesbitt continued to announce the normal progress of the flight.

But everything was not normal. One minute and 13 seconds into the flight of the *Challenger*, the shuttle exploded into a huge fireball. The time was 11:39.13 A.M. Eastern Standard Time. The explosion was so sudden, so totally unexpected that those who were actually witnessing the event could not at first grasp what had happened.

Commander Nesbitt, who was in Houston and only saw the data, had no idea that an explosion had even occurred. One of the most bizarre and haunting images of the disaster was his voice calmly announcing, "One minute 15 seconds. Velocity 2,900 feet per second. Altitude nine nautical miles. Downrange distance seven nautical miles."

By this time it was clear to the spectators at the Cape and to all of those who watched the launch on television that something was terribly wrong. The fireball had been obscured by a cloud of white smoke. The two rocket boosters shot out of the cloud, leaving crazy trails as they plunged toward the ocean. Smaller pieces of smoking debris could be seen falling out of the cloud.

There was a pause of 40 seconds in the announcement from Houston. Then Nesbitt, his voice still calm and unemotional, an-

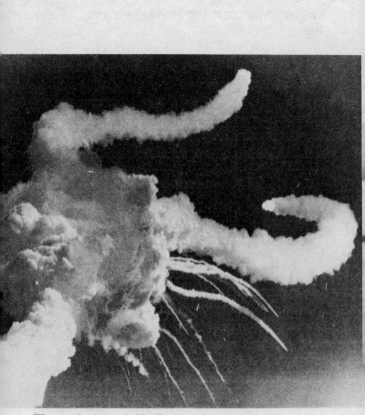

The explosion of *Challenger*. (AP/WIDE WORLD
PHOTOS)

nounced, "Flight controllers are looking very carefully at the situation." After a second he added, what everyone already knew, "Obviously a major malfunction." A few seconds later he continued, "We have no downlink," which meant that there was no more information coming in from *Challenger* for the screens had gone blank. *Challenger* was no more.

As the news of the disaster began to spread, it first reached the newsmen. Dan Rather was in his office in New York, and he raced to the special studio set up for such crises. Tom Brokaw and Peter Jennings, anchors for the other two major networks, were at a White House briefing when they heard the news. Both rushed for their respective Washington studios.

Within minutes after the explosion, all three major networks had broken into regular programming. They stayed on the air nonstop for hours. The tape showing the launch of the shuttle, its steady climb, and then switching to a telephoto close-up just seconds before the explosion, was replayed over and over again.

People heard about the news in a variety of ways. We first heard it about a half hour after the explosion. We called a local business where someone happened to be listening to the radio. "The shuttle just exploded," we were told. Like millions of other Americans when first hearing the news, we turned on a television set, and watched that terrible two-minute clip.

All regular programming on the major networks was pre-empted, and the coverage continued uninterrupted until the evening. By that time virtually everyone in the United States must have heard what had happened. Those who had not been able to get near a television set during the day saw the entire tragedy replayed on the evening news or on special programs later in the night.

There was little additional news that first day. Reporters showed models of the shuttle, described its parts, and explained how it worked, or should have worked. There were interviews with various officials from NASA and others connected with the space program. They didn't have much to say, and seemed as stunned and grief stricken as the rest of us. And that two-minute clip of *Challenger* from lift-off to explosion was repeated again and again. And we watched it until the images were burned permanently into our memory.

Time magazine quoted ABC correspondent Peter Jennings: "We all shared in this experience in an instantaneous way because of television. I can't recall any time or crisis in history when television has had such an impact."

Few would disagree with that assessment. When you remember the *Challenger* tragedy, you will probably remember sitting in front of a TV set.

Another image burned into our collective

memory by the television coverage was the scene at Concord High School, in Concord, New Hampshire, where Christa McAuliffe taught. The students had gathered in the auditorium to watch the long-delayed lift-off on television. The television crews had gathered at the school to watch the students' reaction. There was a party atmosphere at first. Many of the students wore paper hats or tooted horns in anticipation of a celebration of the successful lift-off.

There was cheering when the *Challenger* finally did lift off, but in a little over a minute the cheering stopped, and there was not so much shock as confusion. At first it was not clear to the students what had happened. The voice of Commander Nesbitt seemed to indicate that everything was just fine, yet this contrasted so starkly with the picture of the fireball and smoke on the screen. As the meaning of what happened set in, there was shock and grief. The reaction of the students at Concord was deeper and more personal, but it mirrored the reaction of the rest of the nation and the world.

Chapter 2

THE REACTION

The tragedy had been so sudden, so unexpected, and so stunning that the reaction was slightly delayed. President Ronald Reagan had been scheduled to deliver the State of the Union message that evening. When asked if he would go ahead with the plan, he first had said, "There could be no speech without mentioning this. But you can't stop governing the nation because of a tragedy of this kind. So, yes, one will continue." But then the depth of feeling that the tragedy had stirred began to be recognized. The President put off the State of the Union message for one week. Instead he delivered a brief and moving tribute to the *"Challenger* Seven."

The President was acutely aware of the spe-

Flags around the Washington Monument at half-staff after the *Challenger* accident. The Capitol dome stands in the background. (AP/WIDE WORLD PHOTOS)

cial meaning that *Challenger* had to the nation's schoolchildren. "I know it's hard to understand that sometimes painful things like this happen. It's all part of the process of exploration and discovery. It's all part of taking a chance and expanding man's horizons."

When reporters reached Speaker of the House Tip O'Neill, he seemed stunned, and muttered, "Terrible thing. Terrible thing." In a statement issued later he saluted "those who died performing exploits that people my age grew up reading about in comic books."

Those who had faced the dangers were more stoic. John Glenn, who had been the first American to orbit the earth and is now a senator from Ohio, recalled that the seven original astronauts had often speculated how many of them would be alive after the program. One of them, Virgil "Gus" Grissom died in a 1967 launch pad fire during a test. "We always knew there would be a day like this. We're dealing with speeds and powers and complexities we've never dealt with before. This was a day we wish we could kick back forever."

The legendary test pilot Chuck Yeager, who had risked death aboard experimental aircraft countless times, was the most matter-of-fact. "Watching the film of the shuttle, it shows you how fast and how final things can become. So that's the reason you don't waste time thinking about it." Yeager's tough view was to find out what went wrong, fix it, and get on with the job. Most of us were not that tough. A period of mourning was needed.

All over the nation people groped for ways to express their grief. In Los Angeles, the Olympic torch atop the Memorial Coliseum was lighted. In New York, the lights that normally illuminate the Empire State Building were turned off. In Illinois, people turned their porch lights on; in Miami, thousands shone flashlights skyward. People just wanted to do something, but they weren't quite sure what.

Tributes to the *Challenger* Seven poured in from all over the world. The most interesting, and perhaps most heartfelt tributes, came from the Soviet Union. The Soviets are not just adversaries on the world scene, they are also the only other nation that has a manned space program, and they have had their share of tragedies. Videotapes of *Challenger* were shown on Soviet television and the announcement of what had happened was handled gravely. In tribute, Soviet radio played American music, including the music of Glenn Miller. The band leader Miller had been killed in a plane crash during World War II. Whether the choice of his music at this moment was deliberate or accidental is unknown.

Soviet officials also decided to name two craters on the planet Venus, which had been discovered by Soviet space probes, in honor of

Challenger astronauts Christa McAuliffe and Judith Resnik. By tradition, features of the planet named after the goddess are given women's names only.

On Friday a dignified and incredibly moving memorial service was held at the Johnson Space Center in Houston, Texas. The families of the astronauts and many others who were close to them were present. The principal address was delivered by President Reagan. He ended with these words:

"Dick, Mike, Judy, El, Ron, Greg, and Christa—your families and your country mourn your passing. We bid you good-bye, but we will never forget you."

Chapter 3

CHRISTA McAULIFFE

Suppose for a minute that the shuttle astronauts had been rock stars. They would have been glamorous and great to watch. Crowds would have followed them wherever they went. You probably would have watched them on television just because they were superstars. You probably would have put up posters in your room showing them staring up into the sky. At night you might have dreamed of them. During the day you would have thought of them whenever you got bored, letting your imagination carry you off into a science-fiction adventure starring them. The entire shuttle event would have seemed exciting but unreal like a movie or a video set in outer space.

But it's precisely because the seven members

Christa McAuliffe

of the shuttle crew weren't rock stars or celebrities that their deaths touched us so deeply. When they died in the shuttle explosion, it was as if we had lost a friend, a relative, someone we cared about, someone we knew. No matter how much you admire them, even idealize them, you don't really "know" superstars. They're distant and unreal. It was just the opposite with the members of the *Challenger* crew. They were all very real and very human. Granted just being astronauts made them special and granted they were high achievers. But, basically they were ordinary people and we could see ourselves in them. Take Christa McAuliffe, the teacher-in-space participant and the best known of the *Challenger* crew. She could easily have been a social studies teacher in your own school.

Christa McAuliffe was a warm, friendly, robust, and lively person who lived with her husband, Steve, a lawyer, and her two children, Scott and Caroline, in Concord, New Hampshire. She loved teaching, was an active volunteer in many community organizations, and still found time for hobbies like jogging, tennis, and volleyball. When she was selected by NASA from 11,000 candidates to be the first civilian in space, she was ecstatic. But it also says a lot about Christa McAuliffe that she felt sympathy and concern for the finalists who weren't chosen. On July 19, 1985, at the White House ceremony where Vice-President Bush proclaimed her the winner, she cried and said movingly that though she would carry only one body into space, the souls of all ten finalists would be there riding with her.

The town of Concord went wild over Christa's selection. They made Christa grand marshal of a parade and on New Year's Eve 1985, Concord displayed ice sculptures of rocket ships and stars on the New Hampshire State House lawn. However, fame didn't change Christa McAuliffe. She was still the enthusiastic teacher who kept coming up with new ideas for projects for her students at Concord High School and who planned to go on teaching after the shuttle flight was over. She thought that the choice of a teacher as the first civilian in space would do a lot for the prestige and morale of teachers everywhere and she was proud to represent them.

Perhaps the hardest part about being an astronaut was the time Christa had to spend away from teaching and from her family. Although her interest in people, her hearty optimism, and naturalness made her popular with the public and with reporters, she didn't particularly like being a media star and she did her best to shield her family from all the publicity. What was important to Christa McAuliffe was her husband, her kids, her work, her community, the wonder of space travel, and the good that might come of it, not fame.

She was born to Edward C. and Grace Corrigan in Boston, Massachusetts, on September 2, 1948, the eldest of five children. Although officially her name was Sharon Christa Corrigan, nobody ever called her Sharon. After Christa's father graduated from Boston College, the Corrigan family moved to Framingham, a suburb about 20 miles west of Boston where Mr. Corrigan worked as an accountant. As a child Christa took dancing and piano lessons, but she doesn't appear to have dreamed of becoming a dancer or musician. Instead she opted for a more conventional life. She went to Marian High, a strict Catholic school in Framingham where she got fairly good but not great grades, sang in the glee club, played volleyball and softball, decided to become a teacher and met the man she would one day marry, Steven McAuliffe.

Although it was the era of the '60s and many teenagers were in a rebellious mood, Christa's one act of rebellion in high school was mild. She refused to cover her strapless gown with a jacket at her senior prom even though jackets were the rule. But though she was no rebel, she was open to new ideas. The ideals of John F. Kennedy had a major impact on her life, and in the following decade when the women's liberation movement was in full swing, feminism

Christa training in "zero gravity."

shaped her views in a variety of ways. She was eager to see women face up to new challenges and take advantage of new opportunities, and she worked up a course called "The American Woman" at Concord High School.

When, earlier in her career, she applied for a position as assistant principal at a school and didn't get the job, she wondered if the job was denied her because she was a woman. Even when she was still in college she enjoyed reading the diaries of pioneer women. Later, on her application to NASA she wrote that when she was young, women simply were not allowed to become astronauts, and how much it meant to her for the sake of her female students when Sally Ride and other women began to train as astronauts. Now as the first civilian in space, Christa McAuliffe was about to become a pioneer herself.

When Christa graduated from high school in 1966, she went to Framingham State College, which had mostly women students in those days. She majored in history, getting her B.A. degree in 1970. Shortly afterward she got married. Steven had attended the Virginia Military Institute on an Army scholarship and now he and Christa moved to the Washington, D.C., area so he could study at Georgetown University Law School. Christa taught history to eighth-graders at the Benjamin Foulois Junior High School in Morningside, Maryland. But she soon began teaching at Thomas Johnson Junior High School in Lanham, Maryland. There, from 1971 to 1978, she taught eighth-grade English and American history and ninth-grade civics.

This was a period of Christa's life when she needed every bit of her energy and dynamism. Not only did she teach, but she started working on a master's degree in teaching administration at Bowie State College and worked part-time as a waitress at a Howard Johnson's restaurant to earn extra money. The courses she taught were stimulating and innovative. She took her students on numerous field trips and when it came time to teach them about law she had her classes hold make-believe trials. Christa's first child, Scott Corrigan McAuliffe, was born on September 11, 1976, but by then her husband had finished law school and in 1978 she received her master's degree.

When Steve, who now works for a private law firm, found work as a New Hampshire assistant attorney general, the McAuliffes returned to New England, this time to Concord, where their daughter, Caroline, was born on August 24, 1979. Christa was back teaching by 1980, at a small suburban school called Bow Memorial High School. She taught English to ninth-graders and became president of the teacher's union. In her usual spirited way she kept right on balancing a professional career and a family life, coping with students, her own kids, pet cats, grading homework at night, and keeping the sense of humor for which she was known. Her sense of fun extended to games of Ms. Pac-Man, which she really enjoyed.

In the midst of this busy schedule Christa McAuliffe found time for lots of friends and lots of volunteer work. She was a Girl Scout troop leader, helped with fund-raising for Concord Hospital and the Concord YMCA, belonged to the Junior Service League, taught Christian doctrine classes at St. Peter's Roman Catholic Church, belonged to professional organizations like the New Hampshire Council of Social Studies and the Concord Teachers Association. The McAuliffes were a host family for a Better Chance Program designed for inner-city students.

When Christa's training with NASA grew really intense, her husband stepped in to juggle kids and career alone. This meant a lot of adjustments for Scott and Caroline who were also busy with their own activities, like Scott's hockey team. But if having an astronaut for a mother brought problems, it also brought excitement, and not only for Christa's children but for her wider family, her students at Concord High. On the day of the shuttle launch those students eagerly watched the television screen set up at the school, waiting to see their teacher reach the stars.

Christa planned to hold two 15-minute classes

in space which would be watched by children across the country on closed-circuit television. In addition she would present a tour of the shuttle and describe the work of the crew members. In a way she was a kind of ambassador in space, interpreting for the rest of us the glory of space travel. She wasn't a scientist or technician. She was someone with whom we could identify and understand.

The day of the shuttle launch was her day and ours, and everyone including the Concord High students watched with anticipation as the shuttle sped upward into a bright blue sky. But there would be no lessons, no interpretations. The television screen revealed the awful sight of the exploding shuttle, an explosion that killed Christa McAuliffe and the other astronauts. In the end we can say about Christa McAuliffe that she was a good teacher and a good citizen, and that's a very impressive epitaph. But more than that, she was a nice person, and above all, very real. Her death brought the shuttle tragedy home to the world.

Chapter 4

GREGORY JARVIS

When Gregory Jarvis climbed aboard *Challenger*, he carried a banner from the college he'd graduated from in 1967—the State University of New York (SUNY) at Buffalo. Greg had played football, earned a bachelor of science degree in electrical engineering, and was in the Air Force Reserve Officer Training Corps at Buffalo. It was there that he met Marcia Jarboe of Spring Valley, New York, a suburb not far from New York City. She was a student, too. In June 1968, they got married. Gregory Jarvis felt he owed a lot to SUNY Buffalo. It was at college that the world seemed to open up for him, and he started on the road that finally took him to the space shuttle *Challenger*.

By the time he became an astronaut, Gregory

Jarvis was the kind of man that people call a "go-getter," a "doer," somebody on the move. There were never enough hours in the day for him to accomplish the things he wanted to do and he seemed to possess boundless energy and self-confidence. Yet unlike a lot of "doers," Greg never appeared unpleasantly competitive. He had an engaging personality and people liked him. He was thoughtful. It was Greg who became citizen-in-space astronaut Christa McAuliffe's best friend among the shuttle crew. Unlike several of the shuttle crew members who had already logged hours in space, Gregory Jarvis, like Christa McAuliffe, had never been on a space flight. That gave Greg and Christa something in common. But more than that it was like Greg to reach out a helping hand to someone in a new and scary situation, and he did his best to ease any tensions Christa might have felt about the risks and dangers of space flight.

As an engineer Gregory Jarvis was well aware that something could go wrong with *Challenger.* But he was eager to take part in the launch. Twice before he'd been disappointed when he was dropped from shuttle flights. Originally scheduled to make his debut flight in April 1985 on *Discovery,* he was replaced by Senator Jake Garn of Utah. Greg was also ousted from a launch of the shuttle *Columbia,* losing out to Florida Congressman Bill Nelson.

Gregory Jarvis

So it's hardly surprising that Greg could scarcely wait for *Challenger* to lift off with him aboard. It was the latest challenge in a long series of challenges and Gregory Jarvis had met every one head on.

Gregory Bruce Jarvis was born in Detroit, Michigan, on August 24, 1944, to Bruce and Lucille Jarvis. Greg's father was an accountant who worked for the General Motors Corporation, but when Greg was two his family moved to Mohawk, a small town in Upstate New York. There Gregory's father took over the management of a family-owned drugstore. When he reached his teens, Greg divided his time between studying, working in the drugstore, playing football, managing the basketball team, and playing saxophone in the school band. He also found time to be secretary of the math club and appeared in school plays. Although he had to work hard for it, he made National Honor Society in his senior year.

In contrast to Mohawk, Buffalo is a big city and the University is a big school. But that didn't bother Greg Jarvis. He threw himself into collegiate life with his usual intensity. He continued his interest in athletics. If anything, the interest grew stronger. He and Marcia Jarboe shared a deep love of outdoor sports, such as cross-country skiing, white-water rafting, running in 10-kilometer races, and backpacking. Long after they were out of college and married they toured the Canadian Rockies on a tandem bicycle, covering 65–80 miles a day. Greg's capacity for exercise never declined. Among his favorite hobbies were squash and racquetball. When he needed a break from physical activity, Greg's idea of relaxing was playing classical guitar. He was forever astonishing friends and colleagues by his ability to work all day and engage in hectic physical exercise when work was done. The word "moderation" just wasn't in Gregory Jarvis's vocabulary.

After college Greg went to work for the Raytheon Corporation, in Bedford, Massachusetts, getting a master's degree in electrical engineering in 1969 from Northeastern University in Boston. At this stage of his career his work dealt with the SAM-D missile. Also in 1969 Greg entered active duty in the Air Force and was assigned to the space division in El Segundo, California, where he became a specialist in tactical communications satellites. He rose to the rank of captain, leaving the Air Force in 1973 to join the space and communications group of the Hughes Aircraft Company.

Home for the Jarvises, who had no children, was a yellow stucco house not far from the ocean in Hermosa Beach, a suburb of Los Angeles. Workaholic that he was, Greg devoted himself to his job, which often meant 14-hour days and meetings that started at 6:30 A.M. He attended evening classes at West Coast University in Los Angeles, earning a master's degree in management science. It was to have been awarded him in a special ceremony aboard *Challenger*. As for Marcia, she worked as a dental assistant and continued devoting herself to endurance sports.

Among the many projects Gregory Jarvis worked on was the Leasat satellite developed by the Hughes Aircraft Company. He turned in a superb performance as a manager of the project. So when the Hughes Company was asked by NASA to choose an employee to become part of the shuttle program, the candidate chosen was Greg. He was selected from more than six hundred applicants in 1984. His shuttle mission was to conduct experiments showing the effects of weightlessness on fluids in tanks to see how they move in an orbiting spacecraft.

Gregory Jarvis never got to conduct these experiments and he never experienced the challenge that had come to mean so much to him, the challenge of being an astronaut in space. After the shuttle explosion, the unquenchable spirit of Gregory Jarvis was gone.

Chapter 5

FRANCIS RICHARD SCOBEE

Dick Scobee, as he was called, was born in the town of Cle Elum in Washington. Cle Elum is an Indian name meaning "swift water." A name meaning "steady river" would have suited Dick Scobee better. He wasn't showy, flashy, or quick. He had to work hard in school to keep up his grades. Although he played football, he was slow, showing no special athletic talent. He wasn't particularly popular with girls. He didn't date much in high school, but hung around with a group of guys when he wasn't working part-time at a supermarket. Most people assumed that Dick would get a job on the railroad after he got out of high school, maybe become an engineer on a train like his father. But Dick Scobee would surprise friends and relatives alike with his persistence, taking to the skies and becoming, of all things, a space shuttle pilot. Before his death on *Challenger,* Dick Scobee had logged no less than 168 hours in space.

How did an average person like Dick Scobee manage to achieve such an extraordinary career? He did it by being a lot like the tortoise in the famous folk tale of the tortoise and the hare. Dick Scobee was solid, dependable, patient, and determined. It was these traits that made him a winner.

Francis Richard Scobee was born on May 19, 1939, the eldest of two sons of Francis W. Scobee and his wife, Edie. Dick was raised in the town of Auburn, near Mount Ranier, between Seattle and Tacoma. His father worked for the Northern Pacific Railroad.

From the time he was a kid Dick loved airplanes. Even in elementary school whenever he had a free minute he'd draw pictures of planes. When he was a child, World War II raged across Europe and the Pacific and he filled his room at home with model planes of that era, spitfires and P-38s. When he was in high school, few realized how deeply committed Dick Scobee was to flying. If anything, he seemed unambitious. Since he wasn't a jock superstar he was easily overlooked. But those who took the time and trouble to watch him saw he never quit. A lineman on the Auburn High

Francis "Dick" Scobee

School football team, the Trojans, and a member of the track team, Dick was always quietly there when needed, doing his job.

When he graduated from high school in 1957, Dick didn't talk about how much he wished he could go to the United States Air Force Academy. The academy offered the quickest and surest route to the career about which he dreamed, but he believed he had no way of getting in. So he simply enlisted in the Air Force where he was trained as a mechanic, repairing engines on C-124 cargo planes. At age twenty, while stationed at Kelly Air Force Base in San Antonio, Texas, he met a sixteen-year-old girl named June Kent at a Baptist church hay ride. Within a few months Dick Scobee and June Kent were married.

The persistence that would lead Dick Scobee into space surfaced when he attended night school in San Antonio, earning two years of college credit. Due, in part, to these credits he was admitted to the Airman's Education and Commission Program. In 1965 he received a bachelor of science degree in aerospace engineering from the University of Arizona. Commissioned as a second lieutenant in 1965, he won his Air Force wings in 1966.

Once Dick became a pilot, June went to college. By now the Scobees were the parents of two children, a daughter, Kathie, born on January 30, 1961, and a son, Richard, born on April

13, 1964. Richard would grow up to achieve one of his father's unrealized ambitions: acceptance into the United States Air Force Academy. June's thirst for education led her all the way to a doctorate degree from Texas A & M University and a position as visiting assistant professor of education at the University of Houston, Clear Lake, which is near the Johnson Space Center.

Over the years that followed, Dick Scobee logged more than 6,500 hours flying time in 45 types of aircraft, including the Caribou C-7, which he flew on combat missions in Vietnam from 1968 to 1969. In 1972 he completed training at the Air Force Aerospace Research Pilot School at Edwards Air Force Base and became a test pilot, flying many kinds of aircraft, such as the F-111 transonic tactical bomber, the C-5 cargo jet, the Boeing 747 jumbo jet and the experimental X-24-B, which was the forerunner of the space shuttle.

In 1978 Dick was selected as an astronaut candidate. After completing his training, he was also assigned as an instructor pilot on the NASA Boeing 747 shuttle carrier airplane, which carried the shuttle between ground stations. It was five years before the moment came when Dick Scobee got his big chance. On April 6, 1984, *Challenger* launched from the Kennedy Space Center with Dick Scobee as pilot. The shuttle crew retrieved a broken Solar Max

The shuttle crew that repaired a satellite in space.
Dick Scobee is on the left.

satellite and repaired it on board *Challenger*. Later it was put back in orbit. At a press conference, while still in flight, Scobee and the other astronauts aboard *Challenger* wore T-shirts with the inscription: "Ace Satellite Repair Co." The duration of the shuttle mission was seven days.

It seemed that Dick Scobee could never get enough flight time. Among his hobbies, which included woodworking, motorcycling, racquetball, jogging, and a variety of outdoor sports, was oil painting and what he loved to paint was jet planes. He was co-owner of a two-seat, open-cockpit Starduster 2 stunt plane and his idea of recreation was to fly it cross-country, somersaulting occasionally. He was used to risking his life in the sky. Facing death as an astronaut on a mission was something he understood and accepted with quiet courage.

Chapter 6

MICHAEL J. SMITH

Michael Smith was a farm boy from a small town in North Carolina. Soaring over the Outer Banks, a small group of narrow islands and peninsulas which tinge the Atlantic Ocean off North Carolina, gave him his greatest happiness when he was a teenager. As a child, living across the road from a small airport, he spent a lot of time watching planes take off and land, and he even made a wooden swing for himself in the shape of an airplane. He sold chickens and eggs to make enough money to take flying lessons. He completed his first solo flight the day he turned sixteen, getting his pilot's license before his driver's license. Once, as quarterback of his high-school football team, he called a time-out during a game just to stare up at a large plane overhead. His younger brother, Patrick, shared Mike's fascination with flying, and later became a jet pilot. But Mike had a stronger and more compelling ambition. He wanted to be an astronaut, and without hesitation he set out to reach that goal.

Michael John Smith was born on April 30, 1945, in Beaufort, North Carolina. Hard work on the family's thirteen-acre chicken farm made him physically strong, and in high school he was a star athlete. Mike was captain of the Sea Dogs, the Beaufort High School (now called Carteret High) football team, which under his guidance took a state championship. Mike also played baseball and basketball, was voted most outstanding senior, was president of the Beaufort High student council, and graduated with honors. Reading biographies of astronauts was a hobby, and he noted that most astronauts began as pilots in the armed forces or as test pilots. He also noted that astronauts usually had combat experience. Mike was sixteen when Alan Shepard became America's first man in space and he adopted Shepard as his personal hero. Mike set his sites on the United States Naval Academy at Annapolis as the best place to begin the path that would lead to space. In high school he worked extra hard on math and science, an astronaut's essential tools.

Mike's personality was a plus. He was enthusiastic, confident, and friendly. He made friends

Michael Smith

easily. Mike received an appointment to the United States Naval Academy in June 1963, following his graduation from high school. He graduated from the Naval Academy in 1967, 108th in a class of 893. Shortly afterward he married Jane Anne Jarell, who was from Charlotte, North Carolina. Their first child, Scott, was born on January 12, 1969, then came Alison, born on June 21, 1971, and Erin, their third child, who was born on August 2, 1977.

Mike attended the United States Naval Postgraduate School at Monterey, California, then completed Navy aviation jet training in Kingsville, Texas. He was assigned to the Advanced Jet Training Command, serving as an instructor from May 1969 to March 1971. He flew 225 combat missions during the Vietnam War, winning a number of medals. His plane was hit several times but he wasn't injured. Training at the Naval Test Pilot School followed. He completed his training in 1974 and was assigned to the Strike Aircraft Test Directorate at Patuxent River, Maryland, where he worked on guidance systems for cruise missiles and later taught. He completed two carrier tours in the Mediterranean.

Mike was an amazingly good pilot and incredibly brave. In the spring of 1980 he was selected by NASA to become an astronaut. In order to enter the space program Mike had to turn down the chance to become the commanding officer of an A-6 squadron. Commander Michael J. Smith made his choice and he and his family set off for Houston. He had achieved the goal he had set for himself back in high school, which he had worked toward unswervingly ever since.

Mike knew all about danger. He had risked his life often. When death did come, he was doing what he loved most. He was where he belonged, in the sky.

Chapter 7

RONALD McNAIR

Ronald McNair went from the cotton fields of South Carolina to the stars. It was a tough journey. The odds were against him. But he triumphed, winning shining honors along the way. Ron earned a bachelor of science degree in physics at North Carolina A & T State University, graduating magna cum laude in 1971. In 1976 he received a doctorate in physics from the prestigious Massachusetts Institute of Technology where he worked on the development of lasers. He was named a Presidential Scholar, a Ford Foundation Fellow, won the Omega Psi Phi Scholar of the Year award in 1975, and won the National Society of Black Professional Engineers Distinguished National Scientist award in 1979. Toss in an AAU karate gold medal won in 1976 and five regional black-belt karate championships and you can see that Ron McNair was a very high achiever indeed. A fifth-degree black-belt karate instructor and performing jazz saxophonist, Ron's other interests included running, boxing, football, and cooking.

Ron McNair's achievements are all the more impressive when you consider that he grew up in a small town in South Carolina at a time when the Ku Klux Klan was a powerful force in many rural communities and there didn't seem to be much of a future to strive for if you were black. Talent, initiative, and drive were important factors in Ron's success but so was his strong and supportive family, which cared deeply about education. When new opportunities arose for black students, Ron McNair made full use of them.

Ronald Erwin McNair was born to Carl C. and Pearl M. McNair in Lake City, South Carolina, on October 21, 1950. Ron and his older brother Carl and younger brother Eric grew up in a rustic frame house. Ron's grandfather had been a bishop of the Church of God and religion was central in the McNair household. In that era of segregation, when the law decreed white children attend one school and black students another, Ron's mother was a teacher in a black school. His father was an automobile mechanic who never finished high

Ronald McNair

school and who therefore was all the more eager to see his sons have an education. Ron's grandmother, Mabel Montgomery, valued education so highly that she returned to school late in life, earning a high-school diploma when she was 65.

Although formal schooling began for Ron at four, he learned to read at home at three. Later his family invested in an encyclopedia so he and his brothers could put in extra time studying when school was out and their regular homework finished. In high school Ron was a star baseball player. He also played basketball and football, and sax in the school band. He earned four dollars a day picking cotton, back-breaking work, but he needed the money. He graduated from Carver High School in 1967, valedictorian of his class, and won a scholarship to North Carolina Agricultural and Technical State University at Greensboro. The civil rights movement was in full swing by then, and among Ron's classmates was future civil rights leader and presidential aspirant Jesse Jackson. Although Ron began college as a music major, his counselor urged him to consider a career in engineering instead, and he was accepted to a special program at M.I.T., returning there as a graduate student. The academic competition was fierce, and Ron struggled to overcome gaps in his knowledge. But he applied all his energy and intellect to learning and caught up with

Ronald McNair

students who had entered graduate school better prepared.

While in graduate school he met Cheryl Moore of Queens, New York, and they married. On February 12, 1982, their son, Reginald Ervin, was born and on July 20, 1984, they became the parents of a daughter, Joy Cheray. Following graduation from M.I.T., Ron became a staff physicist with Hughes Research Laboratories in Malibu, California. His work there included research on lasers for satellite-to-satellite space communications. He learned that NASA was looking for scientists in 1977, and in 1978 he was accepted into the space program. The McNairs moved to Houston.

Ron McNair was a mission specialist on a *Challenger* flight in February 1984, logging 191 hours in space. Although being an astronaut was important to him, at heart he was earthbound with roots running deep into South Carolina soil. Ron remained extremely close to his family, including his brothers, also successful high achievers, living in Atlanta, Georgia.

Concerned about social issues and educational opportunities, Ron spoke frequently before state legislatures, urging that money be given to inner-city schools. He also visited classrooms, encouraging children to study hard and stay in school. Before his second *Challenger* mission he visited the University of South Carolina where he was considering taking a position with the engineering school. Although Ronald McNair could have been a celebrity, living anywhere he pleased and moving in the most glamorous of circles, he wanted to go back home. He believed he had a contribution to make to education in the South. The *Challenger* explosion robbed him of that chance but his legacy remains.

Chapter 8

JUDITH RESNIK

Astronaut Judith Resnik, who received a doctorate in electrical engineering from the University of Maryland in 1977, was a gourmet cook, a classical pianist, and a brilliant student. In high school she earned a perfect score of 1600 on her SATs. She had the distinction of being the third woman in space, preceded only by Valentina Tereshkova of the Soviet Union in 1963 and America's Sally Ride in 1983.

Judith loved state-of-the-art equipment and solving complex technical problems. That's why she decided to become an astronaut. To those who knew her, it seemed a surprising choice. Quiet and intense, with great powers of concentration, she was the kind of person you'd expect to find on the faculty of a university or the staff

Judith Resnik

of a research laboratory rather than as a crew member on a space shuttle. Although she enjoyed running, bicycling, and was on the verge of receiving a pilot's license, she wasn't the athletic, outgoing type astronauts so often seem to be.

But Judith Resnik was a complex and private person with a mind of her own. When something caught her imagination she went after it. Being an astronaut intrigued her and she had the courage and drive to reach her goal. In 1977 she filled out an application for NASA, and in 1978 she was accepted, chosen from more than eight thousand applicants. A mission specialist on the maiden flight of *Discovery*, launched from Kennedy Space Center on August 30, 1984, her duties included operating the spacecraft's remote-control arm and conducting experiments with solar energy instruments. At the conclusion of the flight she had logged over 144 hours in space and felt terrific.

Judith Arlene Resnik was born on April 5, 1949, in Akron, Ohio. Her parents divorced when she was seventeen and she decided to live with her father, an optometrist who still resides in Akron. Sarah Polen Belfer, Judith's mother, lives in Cleveland. Judith's younger brother, Charles, is a radiologist living in Richmond, Virginia. As a child Judith attended Hebrew school at Beth El Synagogue and was Bas Mitzvahed there. She graduated from Firestone

High School in Akron in 1966, valedictorian of her class.

Math was Judith's favorite subject in high school, and she excelled in solid geometry and calculus in an age when girls rarely studied math. There were fifteen boys in the math club, but she was the only girl. Judith was a member of the honor society, the French club, and the chemistry club. Although she was wooed by many colleges, she chose Carnegie-Mellon University in Pittsburgh, which was then called Carnegie Tech. She began her college studies as a math major but rapidly switched to engineering because it was the practical aspects of science which most interested her. True to form, Judith graduated in the top five in engineering. Her achievement is all the more impressive because very few women chose engineering as a career at that time. All these glittering academic achievements make Judith sound very serious. But she had a good sense of humor. She had close friends at Carnegie-Mellon, and one year she was even elected runner-up to the homecoming queen. Active in campus organizations, including the sorority Alpha Epsilon Phi, she was on the student advisory committee of the engineering department. It was at Carnegie-Mellon that she met her future husband, Michael Oldak, an engineering student, too.

Judith married Michael after they graduated

Judith Resnik

from college in 1970, and they both went to work for the Radio Corporation of America in Moorestown, New Jersey, near Philadelphia, Pennsylvania. When her husband decided to become a lawyer and was accepted to Georgetown University Law School in Washington, D.C., in 1971, it was time to move. Judith continued working for RCA at a regional office in Springfield, Virginia, and studied for her doctorate.

In 1975 Judith and Michael divorced. By then Judith was a biomedical engineer and staff fellow in the Laboratory of Neurophysiology at the National Institutes of Health in Bethesda, Maryland. Next, it was on to California where she worked for the Xerox Corporation in El Segundo as a senior systems engineer in product development. Despite their divorce, Judith and Michael remained friends, always glad to hear from each other.

Once Judith Resnik became an astronaut the space program became the central focus of her life. She needed purposeful work; to her it gave life meaning. Being an astronaut meant that she could learn about new technologies. She could be part of a team and still find room for individual achievement. On *Challenger* she was supposed to take pictures of Halley's comet. It was the kind of stimulating project she enjoyed. But there was a very warm, very personal side to Judith. She took a ring and locket along on the shuttle to give to a nephew and niece so they could share in her journey through space. On her first shuttle mission she held up a sign that bore the message: "Hi, Dad," an image that was beamed to earth and which meant a lot to her father. Being an astronaut was Judith Resnik's greatest achievement, a source of pride. As far as she was concerned, it was well worth the danger.

Chapter 9

ELLISON S. ONIZUKA

When Ellison Onizuka was a teenager in Hawaii in the early 1960s, he became interested in the Mercury space program. It wasn't the only thing he was interested in. He was in the Boy Scouts, eventually attaining the rank of Eagle Scout. He was a member of the 4-H Club, and played basketball. He also became deeply immersed in Buddhism, the religion of his ancestors. He was a moderately good student but no whiz kid in high school. He liked climbing mountains and poking about in caves, and tinkering with gadgets, trying to figure out how they worked. He was a gentle, modest kind of person, a genuinely nice guy.

Even though he loved to look up at the stars through a telescope at Honolulu's Bishop Mu-

Ellison Onizuka

seum, becoming an astronaut must have seemed an impossible dream to Ellison. Astronauts were white middle-class Protestant males from America's Midwest. All Ellison had to do was look at a picture of the astronauts in a newspaper or watch them on television to see that he had no chance. He was the grandson of Japanese immigrants who found work on the sugar plantations of Hawaii. He'd worked in the fields picking coffee beans, and he helped out in the general store his family owned, which his elderly mother, Mitsue Onizuka, still runs today. But times change and Ellison allowed himself to dream.

In 1978 he was selected by NASA to become one of a class of 35 who would undergo astronaut training. His future stretched skyward after all and he achieved a lofty triple first: becoming the first Hawaiian, the first Japanese-American, and the first Buddhist astronaut.

Ellison Shoji Onizuka was born on June 24, 1946, in the village of Kealakekua on the Kona coast of Hawaii, the third of four children born to Masimitsu and Mitsue Onizuka. Ellison graduated from Konawaena High School in Kealakekua in 1964, then left the islands to attend the University of Colorado in Boulder, studying aerospace engineering as a member of the Air Force Reserve Office Training Corps. He received a bachelor of science degree and a master of science degree in 1969, the year he married Lorna Leiko Yoshida of Pahala, Hawaii, who was also studying in Colorado at a nearby college.

The first of their two daughters, Janelle Mitsue, was born on October 22, 1969. Their second daughter, Darien Lei Sizue, was born on March 11, 1975. In 1970 Ellison Onizuka entered active duty with the United States Air Force and became an aerospace flight test engineer with the Sacramento Air Logistics Center at McClellan Air Force Base near Sacramento, California. Eight exciting years as a test pilot and flight engineer followed. Despite his gentle personality, Ellison was hard-working and ambitious, never one to let opportunities slip by. He had a positive outlook on life. He applied to the elite Air Force test pilot school at Edwards Air Force Base, was accepted, and stayed on to become an instructor teaching students both in the classroom and in the air.

In 1978, when Ellison's training as an astronaut began, the Onizuka family moved near the Johnson Space Center in Houston. In August 1979 Ellison became eligible for assignment as a mission specialist on space shuttle flight crews. He worked on orbiter test and checkout teams and launch support crews at the Kennedy Space Center. He was on the software test and checkout crew at the Shuttle Avionics and Integration

Laboratory (SAIL). His technical assignments ranged from astronaut crew equipment/orbiter crew compartment coordinator to systems and payload development. Ellison was a mission specialist on the first space shuttle Department of Defense mission, launched from Kennedy Space Center on January 24, 1985. At the completion of this flight, Onizuka had logged a total of 74 hours in space.

His success as an astronaut made him a hero, especially to Japanese-Americans, Buddhists, and residents of his home state, Hawaii. He was proud of his heritage. Several years ago he journeyed to his family's ancestral gravesite in Japan. In September 1985 he presented a medallion with a wisteria blossom symbolizing his faith in the Jodo Shinshu branch of Buddhism to the Abbot of Jodo Shinshu Buddhism. Onizuka had worn the medallion on his earlier shuttle mission. In the same year he was grand marshal of Nisei Week festivities in Los Angeles, a major Japanese-American cultural festival. He went back to Hawaii often, visiting friends and relatives, returning with Kona coffee beans, pineapples, and macadamia nuts for engineers and pilots at Mission Control.

He was a family man who liked to work on his house and his car, or watch his daughters play soccer at school. He enjoyed deep-sea fishing. His favorite form of exercise was to run ten miles a day. He could face death bravely because his life had been rich and full. Ellison Onizuka had seen his wildest dreams come true before he so much as climbed aboard *Challenger*. What more can you ask of life than that?

Chapter 10

WHAT WENT WRONG?

At the moment that these words were written, just what caused the *Challenger* tragedy was still unknown. Several different investigations are attempting to zero in on the cause. They may reach a definite conclusion, or the exact cause of the disaster may never be fully agreed upon. But the main outlines are quite clear.

The part of the shuttle that goes into orbit—called, appropriately enough, the orbiter—is the winged vehicle where the crew sits and which carries the satellites and whatever else is taken into space. The orbiter is launched into space atop three huge fuel tanks that provide the power to push the craft beyond earth's gravity.

The largest of the tanks, much larger than the

NASA-S-73-2393

SPACE SHUTTLE MISSION PROFILE

Diagram of a typical space shuttle mission, from lift-off *(lower left)* through orbit, landing, and refitting for future mission.

orbiter itself, contains a highly volatile mixture of liquid hydrogen and liquid oxygen stored at supercold temperatures. This tank supplies the fuel for the orbiter's three main engines. The fuel is routed into the engines through steel and aluminum pipes.

But the main engines don't provide enough thrust to put the craft into orbit. For additional power the shuttle uses two large solid-fuel booster rockets. These boosters are attached to the sides of the liquid fuel tank.

As the launch begins both the main engines and the solid-fuel rockets ignite. It is an awesome sight as the shuttle rises slowly from the launch pad atop a tower of flame. The shuttle needs its maximum power early in the flight. The solid-fuel boosters soon burn out. Then the casings which held the solid fuel are separated from the liquid fuel tank. They are parachuted into the ocean, where they are picked up and can be reused in a later flight.

Shortly before orbit is reached, the large main tank also separates from the orbiter and falls back into the ocean. During orbit and reentry the orbiter itself needs relatively little power.

The *Challenger* disaster occurred when the huge tank containing the highly volatile mixture of liquid gases exploded. In that brief tape of the *Challenger* from lift-off to explosion, we all

Lift-off of *Challenger* in 1983.

saw the fireball and a great cloud of white smoke. Out of the cloud emerged two objects, each leaving its own trail of smoke. These objects were the two solid fuel rocket boosters, blown away from the main body of the shuttle by the blast.

The orbiter itself and its crew didn't stand a chance. It all happened too quickly, too unexpectedly to do anything. There had been no hint of trouble, either aboard the shuttle, back on the ground at Cape Canaveral, or at Mission Control in Houston. Even if there had been some warning, there was no way to separate the orbiter from the liquid-fuel tank, to which it was attached, quickly enough to avoid the disaster.

The question then is not what happened, but why? Why did the liquid-fuel tank explode?

As soon as the shock subsided, the investigations into the causes of the tragedy began. The first task was to pick up as much debris as possible from the explosion. There was never a hope that any of the crew could have survived the catastrophe. The standard procedure in airplane crashes and accidents of this type is to try to piece together as much of the vehicle as possible in order to find clues to the cause of the accident.

In this case the most important clues came from photographs and videotapes. The videotape of the launch that we all saw showed what appeared to be a small plume of flame between the right booster rocket and the large fuel tank, just fractions of a second before the big explosion. Other close-up pictures of the launch indicated a puff of smoke coming from the right booster rocket almost immediately after the engines were ignited.

Most suspicion was immediately centered on the rubber seals, called O-rings, between the separate parts of the right rocket booster. If somehow one of the seals failed and the burning fuel leaked out, coming into contact with the liquid-fuel tank, the result could be an explosion. Or the burning fuel could have pushed the booster into the liquid-fuel tank, causing it to rupture.

But solid-fuel booster rockets had been used successfully many times before. The seals had been extensively tested. Why would one of them suddenly fail? Was there anything unusual about this particular flight?

The answer was yes, the temperature at launch time was below freezing, colder than it had ever been for any previous launch. Just before the launch, the major fear of NASA officials had been a build-up of ice on the shuttle, because ice could damage the protective tiles. The launch was delayed two hours, mainly to allow the ice to melt. When the shuttle was examined at 11 A.M., it was decided that the ice danger no longer existed, and the temperature was rising. So the decision to go ahead with the launch was made.

Investigators began finding some surprising and disturbing information. It turned out that there had been some problems with the O-rings on previous flights. On a couple of occasions, when the boosters were recovered, these rings were found to have been partially burned through. The burns were not severe enough to allow any of the fuel to leak out, but it was a bad sign. There had been some talk of redesigning the solid-fuel booster tanks, but nothing was done.

There was an even more serious revelation. On the night before the flight some engineers from the company that made the rocket boosters told space agency officials the flight should be delayed. They were worried about the effects of the cold on the rubber rings. The engineers felt that the low temperatures would make the rings stiff and more likely to fail. However, the launch was approved anyway.

There was also an indication that sensors on the rocket boosters recorded that during the chilly night before the launch temperatures on the booster had fallen as low as 7°F, far lower than the air temperature. For some reason, not yet determined, these very low readings were ignored. The information wasn't even passed on to the officials who made the final launch decision.

There was also some evidence that one of the O-rings on the right booster had been damaged when the booster was being put together.

Beyond the immediate question of exactly what caused the *Challenger* explosion, the investigations have raised a whole host of questions about how NASA makes its decisions. Why were some of the top NASA officials not even aware that there had been problems with the O-rings and serious objections to launching the *Challenger* in such low temperatures?

One big question lurking in the background is: Was the space agency under too much pressure to meet its ambitious shuttle launch schedule? Although no one has ever suggested that space agency officials deliberately ignored problems that might have risked the lives of the *Challenger* crew, the pressure to get the shuttle off on time might have caused some people not to be as careful as they might have been under less-pressured circumstances. If they believed a problem was a minor one, they might have overlooked it in order to meet the schedule. It is an all-too-human reaction. There can never be complete assurance that everything will work perfectly. If perfect conditions were required, then no space flight would ever be launched. In the end the decision to launch or delay is a human judgment in which an enormous number of factors must be weighed. Was the need to meet a schedule weighed too heavily?

Another problem may have been caused by budget cutbacks. NASA has fewer employees than in the big-budget days of the Apollo program. Many of those who ran the Apollo program have retired or moved on to other jobs, so that the employees are not only fewer in number but less experienced. A lot of the decision-making has been left in the hands of outside contractors—the companies that actually build the various parts of the rockets and spacecraft. In past NASA accidents it was discovered that the work of these contractors was sometimes not as carefully done as it should have been.

The astronauts themselves have been playing a leading role in the investigation of the *Challenger* tragedy. That is only proper, for not only do astronauts' lives depend on the safety of the equipment they ride into orbit, they are, for the most part, highly trained engineers and scientists. They know the shuttle and other spacecraft better than anyone else. Neil Armstrong, the first man on the moon, was appointed vice chairman of the special Presidential panel that was set up to investigate the explosion. Armstrong has retired from spaceflight, but also on the panel is Dr. Sally K. Ride, America's first woman in space, and still an active astronaut. She was highly visible during the investigation, asking some of the toughest questions.

At the Kennedy Space Center, Captain Robert L. Crippin, who piloted the first shuttle into space in 1981, was the official in charge of the operations to find and salvage the *Challenger*'s debris. But, according to *The New York Times:* "Unofficially, he is said to determine virtually every aspect of the inquiry. . . ." Former astronaut Richard H. Truly was head of NASA's own investigation.

NASA's image as an agency that can perform technical miracles has suffered badly. A major shakeup in the agency is underway. Many of the procedures will probably be changed as well. Changes are inevitable after a major disaster.

The investigators have also squabbled among themselves. There have been some charges and counter charges, and many ugly moments with more to come. This, too, is probably inevitable.

Although the space agency is in for some rough times, support in Congress remains solid despite the criticism, the cost, and the dangers. And poll after poll shows that as far as the American public is concerned, support for a strong and continuing space program is overwhelming.

Chapter 11

IT HAS HAPPENED BEFORE

The *Challenger* tragedy was the worst in the history of the United States space program, but there have been other tragedies here and in the Soviet Union. The *Challenger* astronauts, indeed anyone who agrees to go into space, knows the risks, because they know the history. They have agreed to accept these risks. The rest of us need to be reminded that there are real dangers, and that those who accept the dangers are all heroes. In the words of the author Tom Wolfe, they have "the courage to sit on top of a Roman candle . . . and wait for somebody to ignite it."

In the very early days of the U.S. space program, the risks seemed clearer. In the year preceding the first suborbital flight by astronaut

Alan Shepard, the Atlas rocket and the Mercury capsule it carried blew up or had to be blown up by remote control three times in tests. On July 29, 1960, the seven Mercury astronauts watched the rocket carrying a test capsule explode right over their heads. The tests were all unmanned, but the dangers of the system were terribly obvious. So when Shepard blasted off on May 5, 1961, the world held its breath. That flight was near perfect.

There were no deaths in the Mercury or Gemini manned spaceflight programs, though there had been problems. The first deaths in the space program took place not in space but during a ground test. On January 27, 1967, a fire broke out in the Apollo spacecraft as it sat atop its Saturn rocket during a test at Cape Kennedy. Killed were Virgil "Gus" Grissom, Edward White, and Roger Chaffee. The fire began in a short circuit and blazed up furiously in the pure oxygen atmosphere in the Apollo capsule.

Ironically, the astronauts might have been able to escape the fire if the capsule had been fitted with explosive bolts that would blow the hatch open in case of emergency. Years earlier, however, this safety feature had nearly resulted in Grissom's death. He was one of the original Mercury astronauts and his capsule had splashed down into the Atlantic. The explosive bolts blew the hatch open prematurely, and the capsule filled with water, nearly drowning Grissom. After that near miss the system was changed and the explosive bolts abandoned. No system could provide 100 percent safety.

The closest thing to a disaster in space for the United States came on April 13, 1970, when an oxygen tank on *Apollo 13* burst, while the craft was headed toward the moon. The lives of the three astronauts, Captain James A. Lovell, Jr. of the Navy and John L. Swigert, Jr. and Fred W. Halse, Jr., both civilians, were in extreme jeopardy. A landing on the moon, which had been planned was, of course, out of the question. But the damaged craft could not suddenly turn in space and come back to earth. It had to circle the moon before it could return. During the flight the systems aboard *Apollo 13* began to fail for lack of power. The astronauts themselves were suffering from cold and dehydration and were becoming disoriented.

It was only after a magnificent effort by flight controllers and the astronauts themselves, plus some luck, that *Apollo 13* was brought back safely to a splashdown in the ocean. Although the astronauts put on brave faces, they were not in good shape when they were taken from the craft. It had been a very near disaster indeed.

Simply being a military pilot, and most of the early astronauts were military pilots, was a dangerous occupation. Four astronauts were killed in a routine flight in a T-38S, a supersonic fighter. Navy statistics showed that over a 20-year career a pilot had a 23 percent chance of dying in an accident. That did not include combat missions, where death was not considered an accident. Indeed, there are dangers in ordinary life. One astronaut was killed in a car crash.

The Soviet space program has also had its share of tragedies. There have been repeated rumors that Soviet cosmonauts have died in orbit. Such rumors are unconfirmed and probably untrue. However, just three months after the Apollo fire, Colonel Vladimir Komarov was killed when the parachute that was to bring his *Soyuz 1* craft softly back to earth from orbit, became snarled. The craft plunged four miles to the ground.

In June 1971 three cosmonauts—Georgi Dobrovolsky, Vladislav Volkov, and Viktor Patsayev—were found dead when their capsule returned to earth from the *Salyut 1* space station. Apparently, as the capsule that was to bring the cosmonauts back to earth separated from the space station, a valve accidentally opened and the cabin depressurized, suffocating the men.

The dangers of being a test pilot are the same in the Soviet Union. Cosmonaut Yuri Gagarin, the first man to orbit the earth, was killed on March 27, 1968, when the experimental plane that he was testing crashed.

Add to these tragedies some other near misses in U.S. spaceflight, including earlier shuttle missions, and one presumes near misses in the Soviet program as well, and it is fair to conclude that going into space remains a high-risk occupation. It is, in Tom Wolfe's words, "out on the edge of a still-raw technology."

So the history of the space program teaches us that going into space remains dangerous. We cannot ignore these dangers and pretend they no longer exist. Going into space is not just another day at the office. But history also teaches us that we are not going to let the dangers stop us.

After the Apollo fire, NASA suspended flights for 21 months, while methods of mini-mizing the fire hazard, and increasing the possi-bility of escape in case of fire were developed. A mere 2½ years after the tragedy came the spectacular landing of *Apollo 11* on the moon.

The Soviets have reacted the same way. After Komarov's death, manned spaceflights were halted for a year and a half while the Soyuz capsule was redesigned. Since then they have remained very active in putting cosmonauts into orbit.

There is absolutely no reason to believe that once the lessons of the *Challenger* tragedy are absorbed the space program will not continue.

Chapter 12

HOW FAR WE HAVE COME

The *Challenger* tragedy has focused attention on the dangers and problems of manned space-flight. That's only half the story, no less than half. The accomplishments of the space program seem near miraculous when you consider that less than a century ago the airplane was an impossible dream. We must put the tragedy into perspective by taking a look at how far we have come, and how fast.

The idea of space travel was first born, or at least expressed, in science fiction. Way back in 1825 Edgar Allan Poe wrote what is considered the first science-fiction story called "Hans Phaal —a Tale." It was about a trip to the moon. Poe had his hero going to the moon in a hot-air balloon. Poe's ideas about space travel were pretty primitive, and he wasn't entirely serious. In 1870 Jules Verne wrote a more realistic story about a trip to the moon, and others followed.

It was a Russian schoolteacher named Konstantin Tsiokovsky who first seriously discussed the possibility of using rockets for travel to other planets. The major early advances in high-altitude rockets were made by the American scientist Robert Goddard. During World War II the Germans developed the V-2 rocket as an effective weapon. After the war both the United States and the Soviet Union developed active rocket programs. Both countries began planning to put artificial satellites into orbit around the earth. The Soviets did this first. On October 4, 1957, they launched a small round satellite called *Sputnik* into orbit. With *Sputnik* the space age officially began.

Sputnik came as a real shock to most Americans, for we had always considered ourselves far ahead of the Soviets in science and technology. Some people even tried to deny that *Sputnik* was really up there. The scientists knew better. *Sputnik* was the spark that really ignited the U.S. space program. Before the Soviet success, space had not been a high-priority goal. Under pressure the United States tried to get something, practically anything, into orbit. At first there were a series of embarrassing failures as rockets blew up on the launch pad or went astray. But by mid-1958 American rockets were regularly putting satellites into orbit.

The Soviets weren't standing still. *Sputnik II*, carrying a live dog, was orbited on November 3, 1957, to test the effects of weightlessness. It was clear the Soviets were thinking about putting more than dogs into space, and so was the United States.

The first American effort to put a man in space was called Project Mercury. Seven men, all military test pilots, were chosen as the first astronauts. They were Walter Schirra, Jr., Donald "Deke" Slayton, John Glenn, Scott Carpenter, Alan Shepard, Virgil "Gus" Grissom, and Gordon Cooper. The seven became instant celebrities, instant heroes. Everyone in America knew their names and faces. They were presented to the public as all-American boys. In reality they were tough, often combat-hardened veterans. They had to be. They had undertaken a dangerous task.

The Mercury program did not begin smoothly. There were failures and delays. These are expected when testing entirely new technology. But the space program was being carried out in an intense glare of publicity. And, though U.S. officials generally tried to deny it, we were, in fact, in a space race with the Soviets. The Soviets had gained enormous international prestige with their successful space program. The United States was rushing to catch up.

The seven original Mercury astronauts. Front row, left to right: Walter Schirra, Donald Slayton, John Glenn, Scott Carpenter. Back row, left to right: Alan Shepard, Virgil Grissom, Gordon Cooper.

The Soviets had no intention of losing their lead. They scored another stunning first when cosmonaut Yuri Alekseyevich Gagarin orbited the earth on April 12, 1961. He was the first man ever to do so. Then a Soviet major, Gherman Titov, was shot into space and successfully circled the globe 17 times. But the U.S. program was on the move. On May 3, 1961, astronaut Alan Shepard made a successful suborbital flight in the tiny Mercury capsule. The next year, on February 20, 1962, freckle-faced and slightly balding John Glenn became the first American to orbit the earth. The success had not been easily gained.

If the Soviet space program had problems before launch, they didn't talk about it. Flights were announced only after they were successful. But the American program was out in the open, and everyone saw and felt the agonizing series of delays and postponements due to weather and technical mishaps.

Through it all, Glenn remained cool. He also had no illusions about the dangers of space-flight. "Experience in dangerous and unexpected situations is even more valuable than good conditioning," Glenn said. "If you have successfully controlled your airplane in an emergency or dealt with an enemy whose prime object is to destroy you, your chances of making the proper decision the next time are increased."

There was little public talk of death in space, though the astronauts often discussed the possibility. Shortly before his flight, Glenn, through a spokesman, issued a statement to the American people urging them to continue to support space exploration even if he should be killed. "He wants you to understand," said the spokesman, "that he and we have reduced the risk as far as humanly possible, but that there is still risk. He recognized the risk, that there could be a malfunction, that something could happen to him. He pointed out that pioneers have faced risks many times before, that Adm. Richard E. Byrd almost died in the Antarctic, but that didn't stop polar exploration."

The flight, however, went off rather smoothly. There were some minor problems. Throughout almost the entire three orbits, there was a lit warning light on the control panel. It might have indicated that the capsule's heat shield was loose, and that could spell disaster during reentry. Glenn and the flight controllers worried. It came to nothing. During reentry the craft wobbled erratically. But the Mercury capsule splashed down in the Atlantic within sight of the recovery ship. Glenn's flight was a major triumph.

In an America hungry for heroes, John Glenn became our biggest American hero since Charles Lindburgh made his solo flight across the Atlantic in 1927. He may have been even a bigger hero. People only read about the Lindburgh flight in their newspapers. Americans were able to follow the progress of Glenn's flight live, on radio and television. When Lindburgh had his traditional ticker-tape parade in Manhattan, 1,750 tons of shredded paper poured down. Glenn got 3,464 tons.

The United States was now fully committed to an active manned space program with the aim of putting an American on the moon. President John F. Kennedy said he believed that goal could be attained by the end of the decade, that is before 1970. To many, that seemed a completely unrealistic goal.

After Mercury, the next step was Gemini, not a moon shot yet, but a larger and more maneuverable two-man craft that would orbit the earth. However, there was to be a delay of two years between the Mercury and Gemini programs. In the meantime the Soviets were still actively pursuing their own space program. On June 14, 1963, the Soviet craft *Vostok VI* with cosmonaut Vladimir Bykovsky aboard blasted into orbit. Two days later *Vostok VII* lifted off, and at the controls was Valentina Tereshkova, who was to be the first woman in space. Before they returned to earth three days later, the two spaceships passed within three miles of one another. The cosmonauts could easily see one another's craft.

In the spring of 1964 the Soviets orbited the

world's first three-man spacecraft, *Voshkod I*. Six months later, another Voshkod spaceship flew into orbit and provided the world with another first. Cosmonaut Alexei Leonov opened the hatch and took the first step into the empty blackness of space. He maneuvered outside the spaceship for ten minutes. This first "space walk" had almost as much impact on the world's imagination as had the first manned spaceflight.

Less than a week after Leonov's space walk and the Soviet's return to earth, the United States flew two men for the first time. Gus Grissom and space rookie John W. Young tested the *Gemini 3* spacecraft for three orbits. They used maneuvering rockets to lower their altitude and nudge the spaceship from side to side, changing the path around the earth.

On June 3, 1965, during the third orbit of *Gemini 3*, astronaut Edward White stepped out of the craft to become the first American to "walk" in space. Spectacular live TV pictures of the twenty-minute "walk in space" were beamed back to earth, and people across the world were glued to their TV sets as they hadn't been since the earliest days of the manned space program.

After the space walk, however, a certain amount of public boredom set in. Project Gemini still had important work to accomplish, particularly the docking of two ships in space.

Successfully completing this maneuver was absolutely essential before a manned moon landing could be attempted. Docking was one of the most difficult feats accomplished in space up to that time. But the public was waiting for the big show, getting a man on the moon. That was the aim of Project Apollo.

The Apollo craft had to be tested, first in orbits around the earth, and then around the moon. On January 27, 1967, while three astronauts were running through a check of the Apollo craft on the launch pad, there was a disastrous fire and the three, veteran Gus Grissom, space-walker Ed White, and rookie astronaut Roger Chaffee, were killed. Months of investigation, criticism, and self-criticism by NASA followed. The question was repeatedly asked: Was the program being pushed too fast? Was the safety of the astronauts being compromised in a rush to meet an artificial deadline? They are the same questions that are being asked about the *Challenger* tragedy.

Design changes were made, and within two years the Apollo program was back on track. The Apollo craft was successfully tested in earth orbit early in 1968. By mid-November, the space agency decided to go for broke with *Apollo 8*. It would fly to the moon, orbit it ten times over the Christmas holidays, and head for home.

The moon had already been orbited and

closely photographed by unmanned craft. But to those of us on earth the views provided by human eyes were somehow more thrilling, more real. Astronaut Frank Borman ended a Christmas telecast from moon orbit with this wish: "And from the crew of *Apollo 8,* we close with good night, good luck, a Merry Christmas, and God bless all of you, all of you on the good earth."

There was still a lot more work to be done. *Apollo 10* orbited the moon. Then the lunar lander separated from the command ship and carried two men down close to the moon's surface. They were to check out future landing sites but not actually land. The lander returned the men to the command ship and the mission headed home.

Apollo was now in high gear, and the Soviet space effort was obviously flagging. At one time there had been speculation that the Russians were going to beat the Americans to the moon. By 1969 they seemed to have dropped out of the moon race entirely.

The big show was scheduled for July 1969, when *Apollo 11* was to land on the moon. The three-man crew was led by Neil Armstrong, who was destined to be the first to touch lunar soil, Edwin Aldrin, who would also ride down in the lunar lander and be the second man to walk on the moon. The third member of the crew was Michael Collins, who had the unspectacular, but absolutely essential job of flying patrol in the command ship orbiting the moon while his two crewmates descended to the surface.

At first it seemed that the American public was not terribly enthusiastic about the idea of going to the moon. One poll indicated that at least half of those questioned weren't in favor of the mission. They thought it wouldn't work, couldn't work, and shouldn't work. But as people realized that it was going to be tried, excitement grew.

On launch day over a million people gathered in the Cape area to catch some glimpse of the lift-off. There had never been a crowd like it for any previous spaceflight. In addition some 500 million people watched the lift-off on television.

The lunar lander, christened *Eagle,* came to rest on the moon's surface at 4:18 P.M. Florida time, Sunday, July 20, 1969. A camera mounted outside of the lander allowed the whole world to view the first careful steps of a man on the moon. Armstrong's boot touched the lunar surface at 10:56, his first words were: "That's one small step for a man, one giant leap for mankind." The transmission was slightly garbled and the message came across: "That's one small step for man, one giant leap for mankind."

It was an event that very few born before the dawn of the space age thought that they would

Edwin Aldrin walking on the moon.

live to see. In 1950 the authors of this book, as teenagers, had seen a popular science-fiction film called *Destination Moon*. Nineteen years later that fiction had become reality and we were watching it live on television.

After that emotional high point the manned space program began to wind down. *Skylab,* a manned space station, was established in 1973. In 1975 there was a link-up in orbit between the U.S. craft *Apollo 18* and the Soviet *Soyuz 19*. What had begun as a competition between the two superpowers had, at least temporarily, been turned into a symbol of international cooperation. There are other manned projects, like a mission to Mars, in the planning stage, but they are far in the future. Since the mid-1970s, the main thrust of America's manned space efforts have centered on the space shuttle.

Chapter 13

WHY A SHUTTLE?

In the afterglow of a successful moon landing, why did the United States scale down its space program? There were other projects that could have been pursued. A permanent manned station in space had been discussed. There was the possibility of establishing bases on the moon. How about a manned mission to Mars? All of these goals were within reach. Why did we settle on a space shuttle as our only active manned space project?

The answer can be given in one word—money.

Space exploration is very, very expensive. The successful Apollo program cost billions of dollars. A moon base or a Mars landing would cost even more. Where would the government get the money? Would other government programs be slashed or abandoned? Would taxes be raised? Where would the money come from?

So the decision was made to cut back the cost of the manned space program. The U.S. program of space exploration would continue, but at a slower, less expensive pace. That's where the space shuttle came in. Such a vehicle has a lot of advantages. First, it's reusable. The Mercury, Gemini, and Apollo vehicles were parachuted into the ocean. Even if they were recovered (and they usually were), they could not be reused. The space shuttle landed like an ordinary airplane. It could be sent back into space on another mission. Obviously that would save a lot of money.

The space shuttle is also versatile. It can perform a lot of different tasks. One of the things that can be done efficiently with the shuttle is launch unmanned satellites. One or more satellites are stored inside the shuttle's large cargo bay. When the shuttle is in orbit it releases the satellites. The shuttle has been used to launch a lot of military surveillance satellites. In fact, the Pentagon has been the shuttle's biggest customer. But private companies have also used the shuttle. The *Challenger* was carrying a communications satellite for the Western Union Company. These companies paid for using the shuttle. It was hoped, that by selling its services the shuttle would, one day, be able to pay for itself or actually make money. The shuttle could also be used to capture and repair damaged satellites in orbit. A million-dollar satellite that had stopped working because of a minor malfunction could be saved.

The shuttle could be used to conduct a variety of scientific experiments. Businesses have also used the shuttle to perform experiments. Some pharmaceutical companies had been testing methods of purifying certain drugs in the weightlessness of space. Other manufacturers had been studying the properties of metals in zero gravity. Companies paid NASA to conduct these experiments aboard the shuttle. This sort of work helped pay the bills. In addition, there were experiments in "pure" science, studying the sun and the planets. These experiments didn't produce any immediate practical results, but they have increased our knowledge of the universe.

Finally, the shuttle kept Americans in space. With the shuttle program the techniques of space travel could be refined and perfected and the experience could be put to use in the future when more ambitious projects like the Mars mission would be launched. The shuttle would be needed for building a space station, and a space station would be needed for planetary exploration.

Like every other space program the shuttle had problems at the start. Originally, NASA had a very ambitious shuttle plan. The agency wanted to build a craft that could land at commercial airports. It was also hoped that there would also be a space "tug" that would boost the shuttle into a much higher orbit. But these plans proved to be too impractical, too expensive.

Even once a plan was decided upon there continued to be problems, mainly with the engines and with the heat-resistant tiles. By 1978 there was some talk of dropping the shuttle project completely. But NASA persisted.

Finally, in 1981, the first space shuttle *Columbia* was launched from Cape Canaveral and after a successful flight, executed a flawless landing at Edwards Air Force Base in California. The American public had seen launchings before, but the graceful, easy landing of a vehicle that had been orbiting the earth was a new and beautiful sight. True enough, the shuttle was already 2½ years behind schedule and about 20 percent over budget, but it worked. People began to get excited about it, as they once had about the Mercury and Apollo programs.

There was something else very attractive about the shuttle: Compared to all previous space vehicles, the shuttle could carry a lot of people. Not everyone who rode the shuttle had to be a highly experienced test pilot, or needed years of special training. This opened the door

The *Challenger* landing in April 1983.

for a greater range of people to go into space. In 1983 astronaut Sally K. Ride became the first American woman to go into space as a member of a shuttle crew. A couple of congressmen rode the shuttle into space. Ride, however, was a trained astronaut and the congressmen had aviation experience. The possibility opened up that an "ordinary citizen," that is, someone with no previous connection with aeronautics and space, could quickly be prepared for a ride aboard the shuttle. That is where the "teacher in space program" came from. Christa McAuliffe was by no means "ordinary," but she was not a professional either.

After the *Columbia,* three other shuttle vehicles—*Discovery, Atlantis,* and *Challenger*—were built and orbited successfully. All together the space shuttle program had 24 successful missions. To the general public, the shuttle success seemed almost routine. Riding the shuttle was like riding the bus to work.

Beneath the placid surface, however, there were still problems. Technical problems of one sort or another often delayed or canceled flights. Sometimes flights were not able to carry out their full missions. No matter how it seemed to the rest of us, the astronauts and everyone else connected with the shuttle program knew full well that a ride in the shuttle was not just like a ride on the bus. It was still a risky and dangerous activity.

The delays and other problems raised the cost of shuttle flights. The shuttle wasn't making money. It wasn't near breaking even. Shuttle critics complained that it was a financial flop. Some of the commercial customers began to worry about the repeated delays, and looked for other ways to get their satellites into space. Many turned to the Europeans who were launching satellites at modest cost with conventional rockets in their *Ariane* program. The shuttle's biggest customer, the Pentagon, was building up its own fleet of conventional rockets for satellite launching. Some in the military didn't think the shuttle was dependable enough.

But NASA hoped that it had finally worked most of the bugs out of the shuttle program and that it could begin flying on a regular basis. A series of 15 shuttle launches had been scheduled for 1986. It was to have been NASA's biggest year since the frantic days of the Apollo program.

Chapter 14

MANNED OR UNMANNED

Just two days before the world watched in horror as the *Challenger* exploded, people were seeing a very different sort of picture from space on their TV screens. The unmanned spacecraft *Voyager 2* was sending back spectacular photos and other data from the vicinity of the planet Uranus. *Voyager* had worked better than anyone could possibly have hoped. In eight years it had explored Jupiter, Saturn, and Uranus, sending back data it will take scientists years to analyze. The spacecraft is now on its way to the planet Neptune. Yet *Voyager* had cost less than $150 million to build. *Challenger* originally cost $1.2 billion to build and several hundred million to operate on each mission.

The contrast between the *Voyager* success,

and the *Challenger* disaster did not go unnoticed. It heated up an old debate over manned versus unmanned spacecraft.

The U.S. space program has always had both. There have been the manned projects, like Apollo, which put a man on the moon. And there have been the unmanned projects, like Viking, which landed an instrument package on Mars to photograph the Martian surface and test the Martian soil.

No one argues that some unmanned spacecraft are necessary. There is no possible way that a manned craft could do what *Voyager* has done. We don't have the technology to send a large craft that far. And we don't have the technology to keep a crew alive in space for a twenty- or thirty-year round trip. We can't put people into a state of suspended animation. That's still science fiction. And there is no "warp drive" either, to make the trip faster. That's science fiction, too.

There are a fair number of scientists who argue that manned spacecraft are not necessary for space exploration. They say that practically anything that can be done in space by a human being can be done better, more cheaply, and far more safely by a robot. A larger, more complicated vehicle is needed to get a human into space and keep him or her alive.

One of the most outspoken opponents of manned spaceflight is Cornell University astronomer Thomas Gold. Just a few days before the *Challenger* tragedy, Dr. Gold appeared on ABC's Nightline broadcast. He praised the *Voyager* success and said that the manned missions could not be justified scientifically or economically. He also said they were dangerous, and the danger could not be justified either. After the *Challenger* explosion, Dr. Gold said bluntly, "The shuttle program should be scrapped."

It isn't that Dr. Gold and others like him think that human beings should never be put into space. It's just that they believe that at the present time it's too expensive and too dangerous. Since the early 1970s many scientists have argued that NASA's emphasis on manned programs, particularly the shuttle, has diverted funds and attention from more interesting and more significant work in space.

Sometimes people even get in the way in space. According to *Newsweek* magazine: "Thomas Donahue, chairman of the Space Science Board of the National Academy of Sciences, notes that man-made vibrations can wreck optical experiments. Similarly an astronaut's sneeze can ruin experiments in microgravity."

Supporters of manned spaceflight counter that there are some things only humans can do. In 1984 an astronaut from *Challenger* was able to repair a faulty scientific satellite that might otherwise have become useless.

Critics, however, remain skeptical of the "repairman in space argument." They point out that engineers on the ground have often been able to fix malfunctioning satellites. There had been problems with *Voyager 2* which had been corrected from the earth. Indeed, the whole course of *Voyager 2* had been radically altered by radio signals.

Simple repairs in space can be done by a robot-controlled arm, and the arm can be controlled as well from earth as from a spacecraft. Finally, it's so expensive to put a manned spacecraft into orbit that it would probably be cheaper to put up another satellite rather than send a crew up to fix the old one.

Robots couldn't put together NASA's planned space station. The station, tentatively scheduled for the early 1990s, would be constructed of prefabricated sections assembled in orbit by astronaut construction workers. The station would then be maintained by a crew of six to eight.

A more immediate argument for manned spaceflight is the Hubble space telescope. This extremely sensitive $1.2 billion piece of equipment is designed to give us our best look ever into deep space to answer questions about the creation of the universe. It is a tremendously exciting space science experiment. Before the *Challenger* disaster the telescope was scheduled to be launched by the shuttle this year. When it is finally launched the telescope will require periodic maintenance by astronauts.

There is also a political argument. Can the United States give up manned space entirely, and leave it to the Soviets? While the Soviets never actively pursued a manned moon landing, they still have a very active manned space program. At present they appear to be most interested in establishing a manned space station.

There has also been a debate over who should ride the shuttle into space. Senator and former astronaut John Glenn is one of those who has consistently opposed the "citizen in space" program, which put Christa McAuliffe aboard *Challenger*. The "teacher in space" was essentially a passenger. She contributed nothing *directly* to the mission. Her role was to make the space program more real, and more attractive to those of us here on earth. A couple of congressmen who were on earlier shuttle flights had the same sort of role. It was good public relations, and helped NASA get the money needed from a budget-conscious Congress.

Glenn and others like him believe that only astronauts who actually run the craft and scientists who are actively conducting experiments should occupy limited spots available on the

Left to right: Gregory Jarvis, Christa McAuliffe, and Barbara Morgan, backup "teacher in space."

very expensive flights. Critics also argue that no matter how many times ordinary citizens were told of the dangers of spaceflight, they would not fully comprehend them.

In the end, the manned versus unmanned argument probably won't be decided on strictly scientific or political grounds. There has always been a deeply emotional side to space travel. Maybe a machine could do it as well, or better, but we want to have people up there to see and to experience the new frontier of space. The frontier has always been an important symbol to Americans. Pioneers have always been our heroes, and a nation needs its heroes. We also want to feel that we, too, could be up there in space. We want someone to identify with. That's why the death of the *Challenger* crew affected us so deeply. They were heroes, but not remote ones. They were heroes we identified with. Without that emotion, we would probably not be willing to support the cost of the space program in this time of tight federal budgets.

So there may be delays and changes in plans for future manned spaceflight, but whatever the expense, and whatever the risks, the manned spaceflight program in the United States will certainly continue.

Chapter 15

THE FUTURE IN SPACE

Trying to anticipate what's going to happen in space exploration in the future is risky. But a few basic trends are quite clear:

1. The shuttle program is going to be delayed. Whether that delay will be a matter of months or years is unknown. Much depends on finding out exactly what went wrong with *Challenger*, then seeing how long it will take to correct the problem. After the Apollo launch-pad fire in 1967 the program was set back for 21 months.

2. No matter what kind of shortcomings are found in the shuttle program, it will continue. We are too deeply committed to the shuttle to abandon it. The military uses of the shuttle alone ensure that the program will continue.

3. Despite the tragedy, our long-term goals in

space remain unchanged, and the future is exciting.

NASA had planned 15 shuttle missions in 1986. To many, that schedule seemed too optimistic, even before the *Challenger* tragedy. Obviously it isn't going to be met. There will be no more shuttle flights this year. There may not be any next year either.

One early casualty was the plan to observe Halley's comet through telescopes aboard the shuttle. Many scientists were already disappointed because our effort to study the comet was so limited. The Soviet Union, Japan and Western Europe had probes that have rendezvoused with Halley's comet, sending back spectacular pictures of the comet. The only major U.S. participation in comet observation was to be the shuttle telescopes. By the time the shuttle flies again, Halley's comet will be gone, not to return for another 76 years.

Shuttle flights were also to deploy two scientific spacecraft—*Ulysses,* a European-American device that would study the sun, and *Galileo,* an American craft that would explore Jupiter. If they are not launched by June, they will have to wait another 13 months before the conditions are again favorable. Some time this year the very sophisticated Hubble space telescope, which is designed to see the edges of the known universe, was due to be launched. The telescope would also have to be serviced from a shuttle.

A lot of commercial communications satellite launches will be delayed. Many of them may, at least temporarily, be transferred to the shuttle's chief competitor, the European *Ariane* rockets. Once lost, that business may not be easy to recover.

The Pentagon is the shuttle's biggest customer. The launching of many military satellites will be delayed. Some will probably be orbited by Titan rockets. The Air Force never believed in relying fully on the shuttle. Extra rockets had been ordered just in case of an emergency like the *Challenger* explosion. (There will be increased emphasis on the use of unmanned rockets to launch satellites.) Still it's unlikely that the rockets will be able to pick up all the shuttle work. When the shuttle gets flying again, there will be a backlog of military satellites to be launched. The Pentagon will probably bump some civilian payloads, and schedules will be disrupted for several years.

Three of this year's planned shuttle missions were to carry military cargos linked to the space-based missile defense system popularly known as "Star Wars." Although the nature of the cargos is top secret, it is possible that some of them could not be launched by presently available conventional rockets. The U.S. military is now so deeply committed to the shuttle that it will certainly block any attempts to end the program. There is simply nothing to take the shuttle's place.

The ambitious shuttle program depended on using four different orbiters. Now there are only three. If a new orbiter is built to replace *Challenger,* it will cost about $2 billion, and take anywhere from three to five years to complete. Will the government want to put that kind of money into a new shuttle? Only time will tell.

There had already been talk of building an updated version of the shuttle, or what has been called a "hypersonic transatmospheric vehicle" that would be able to land at conventional airports. No decisions have been made about any of these plans, but you will certainly be hearing more about them in the near future.

A space station assembled by astronauts from a shuttle is tentatively scheduled for the mid-1990s. The station is planned as a permanent base in space. Men and women would be ferried up to the station where they would work for months at a time. The work would be pure science as well as more practical experiments involving the manufacture of drugs, crystals, and metal alloys under weightless conditions. The space station is also to be the staging place for any future manned exploration of the planets. The craft going to Mars or other planets would have to be assembled in space by astronauts from a space station. The whole concept of a U.S. space station is entirely dependent on a successful shuttle program. Indeed, many feel that the primary reason for having a shuttle at all is so that it can service an orbiting space station. With the Soviets apparently ready to establish their own space station, this might inspire the United States to press forward more energetically in this area.

Immediately after the moon landing, there was a great deal of talk about establishing a permanent base on the moon. The idea raised a host of practical problems, and it is less popular now than it was back in the 1970s. But if any manned lunar station were to be built, the first step would certainly have to be a space station orbiting the earth.

But by far the most exciting manned space mission in the foreseeable future is a manned mission to the planet Mars. The moon landing was an event which amazed and inspired the world. But to land on another planet, particularly Mars—a planet which has always fascinated us—would be even more exciting and more historic.

That adventure is within our grasp. The technology exists today—no breakthroughs are needed. It would be expensive to be sure, but it would not be as expensive as the Apollo program, and it would be far less costly than the planned "Star Wars" program.

Recently, astronomer Carl Sagan made a bold proposal about an expedition to Mars. Sagan had never been a great enthusiast for manned spaceflight. Like many other scientists he felt that the scientific results did not really justify the effort. But recently he suggested in an article in *Parade* magazine that the United States and the Soviet Union plan a joint mission to Mars, starting in 1992. That year, he pointed out, is the 75th anniversary of the Russian Revolution. But even more significantly it is the 500th anniversary of Christopher Columbus's discovery of the New World.

"What could be more fitting for 1992 than the initiation of an international program for the exploration and eventual settlement of another New World?"

The Mars landing would not take place as early as 1992, but by that time both the United States and the Soviet Union could have orbiting space stations, and they could begin assembling the components of the craft that would take people to Mars.

The project is ambitious, and it would be costly. Of course, if both nations shared the expense, that would be an enormous saving for each one.

Said Sagan, "In the long run, the binding up

of the wounds on Earth and the exploration of Mars might go hand in hand, each activity aiding the other. The wonders of Mars will occupy us for a long time. . . ."

Commitments to projects like this, which expand humanity's frontiers in space, would be the most fitting tribute to the heroes of the *Challenger,* and to all those who have been pioneers in space.

JOIN NANCY DREW
AT THE COUNTRY CLUB!

You can be a charter member of Nancy Drew's River Heights Country Club™— Join today! Be a part of the wonderful, exciting and adventurous world of River Heights, USA™.

You'll get four issues of the Country Club's quarterly newsletter with valuable advice from the nation's top experts on make-up, fashion, dating, romance, and how to take charge and plan your future. Plus, you'll get a complete River Heights, USA, Country Club™ membership kit containing an official ID card for your wallet, an 8-inch full color iron-on transfer, a laminated bookmark, 25 sticker seals, and a beautiful enamel pin of the Country Club logo.

It's a retail value of over $12. But, as a charter member, right now you can get in on the action for only $5.00. So, fill out and mail the coupon and a check or money order now. *Please do not send cash.* Then get ready for the most exciting adventure of your life!

MAIL TO: Nancy Drew's River Heights Country Club
House of Hibbert   CN-4609
Trenton, NJ 08650

Here's my check or money order for $5.00! I want to be a charter member of the exciting new Nancy Drew's River Heights, USA Country Club™.

Name _____ Age _____

Address _____

City _____ State _____ ZIP _____

Allow six to eight weeks for delivery.   NDDC6

Created by Rosemary Joyce
The Exciting New Soap-Opera Series

DREAM GIRLS™ is the enchanting new series that has all the glamour of the Miss America Pageant and gives you a chance to share the dreams and schemes of girls competing in beauty pageants.

Here Is Your Chance To Become A
"DREAM GIRL"
Enter NOW!!!
TIGER BEAT® and ARCHWAY'S
"Dream Of A Lifetime"
SWEEPSTAKES/COVER CONTEST

To enter this exciting contest just fill in the entry blank provided and include a photograph.

FIRST PRIZE: One lucky winner will be the model for an upcoming cover of a DREAM GIRLS™ book. The winner will also receive a "Dream Weekend" for two—winner and parent/chaperone—to New York City. Series creator Rosemary Joyce will accompany the winner to a photography session and complete beauty makeover to help launch the winner's portfolio. Photographs of the winner will also be sent to top fashion magazines and modeling agencies.

SECOND PRIZE: 50 BEAUTY PACKS (make-up and perfume)—no photographs required.

THIRD PRIZES: 1,000 of the latest title in the DREAM GIRLS™ series—no photographs required.

The winner of the First Prize will be the person who the judges think best personifies all of the "Dream Girls" qualities. Winners for the Second and Third Prizes will be chosen at random.

Look For DREAM GIRLS™ Books In
Your Local Booksellers YA Section

Don't Miss Your Chance To Be A Winner!

Fill in the entry blank provided below

_____   (   )
(Name)   (Telephone Number)

_____
(Address)   (State)   (Zip Code)

_____
(Age/Grade—optional)

1. No purchase necessary. To enter hand print your name, address, zip code, telephone number and age on the official entry form or on a 3×5 card. Mail the form to Simon & Schuster, Attn: DREAM GIRLS,™ 1230 Avenue of the Americas, 12th floor, New York, NY 10124-006. Entries must be received no later than 11/30/86. No photocopies allowed. One entry per envelope, per person, may be submitted. No responsibility assumed for late, lost or misdirected mail. If you wish to enter the Cover Contest also enclose one full-color photograph of yourself with your name, address and telephone number printed on the back. Photographs will not be returned.

2. All prizes will be awarded. Prizes are non-transferable and non-redeemable for cash. No substitutions allowed. One prize per person, address or household.

3. Winner will be randomly selected from all entries received, with the exception of the Cover Contest. Cover winner, if under the age of 21, will need to provide parent or guardian written consent.

4. Prizes are: to be chosen as a model for the cover of an upcoming DREAM GIRLS™ title. Winner will be flown to New York City for a weekend with one parent or chaperone. Winner will meet with series' creator Rosemary Joyce and will be treated to a beauty makeover and photography session. All expenses covered will be put in writing to the winner and guardian before the trip takes place. Photographs of winner will be sent to fashion magazines and modeling agencies. Retail value depends upon residence of winner, but will be no less than $1,000. 50 Beauty Packs containing make-up and perfume—retail value of approximately $25 each; 1,000 of the latest DREAM GIRLS™ title—retail value: $2.50 each.

5. Prizes must be claimed within 30 days of notification attempt or prize is subject to forfeiture, in which case a substitute winner will be selected.

6. All taxes are the responsibility of the winners. Winners may be required to execute an affidavit for eligibility and release. Winners grant to Simon & Schuster the right to use their names and likenesses on book covers and in advertising and promotion related to the sweepstakes.

7. The odds of winning will be determined by the number of entries received.

8. The sweepstakes is open to all residents of the U.S. except employees and their immediate families of Simon & Schuster and Tiger Beat and their agencies.

9. A list of major prize winners can be obtained by sending a self-addressed stamped envelope to: Winners List, c/o Simon & Schuster, DREAM GIRLS,™ 1230 Avenue of the Americas, 12th floor, New York, NY 10124-006.

DM-CON-2

MEET THE

The exciting new soap-opera series

DREAM GIRLS™ is the enchanting new series that has all the glamour of the Miss America Pageant, the intrigue of Sweet Valley High, and the chance to share the dreams and schemes of girls competing in beauty pageants.

In DREAM GIRLS™ you will meet Linda Ellis, a shy, straightforward beautiful girl entering the fast-paced world of beauty contests. Vying for the limelight with Linda is Arleen McVie who is as aggressive, devious and scheming as she is attractive. Join Linda and Arleen as they compete for the scholarships, the new wardrobes, the prizes, the boyfriends and the glitz of being number one!

Come share the dream as you join the DREAM GIRLS™ backstage in their quest for fame and glory.

**#1 ANYTHING TO WIN
#2 LOVE OR GLORY?
#3 TARNISHED VICTORY
#4 BOND OF LOVE
#5 TOO CLOSE FOR COMFORT
#6 UP TO NO GOOD**

**Archway Paperbacks
Published by Pocket Books,
A Division of Simon & Schuster, Inc.**

414